Good Question!

Where Do Garbage Trucks Go?

AND OTHER QUESTIONS ABOUT. . .

Trash and Recycling

STERLING CHILDREN'S BOOKS
New York

STERLING CHILDREN'S BOOKS
New York

An Imprint of Sterling Publishing
1166 Avenue of the Americas
New York, NY 10036

Text © 2015 Benjamin Richmond
Illustrations © 2015 Sterling Publishing Co., Inc.

Photo credits: 6: The Museum of the City of New York/Art Resource, NY; 9: © Hurst Photo/Shutterstock;
10: © Victor J. Blue/Bloomberg/Getty Images; 17: Thinkstock; 21: © Meinzahn/iStockphoto;
22: © Frances Roberts/Alamy; 26: © antikainen/Thinkstock

ISBN 978-1-4549-1624-6 [hardcover]
ISBN 978-1-4549-1625-3 [paperback]

Distributed in Canada by Sterling Publishing
c/o Canadian Manda Group, 664 Annette Street
Toronto, Ontario, Canada M6S 2C8
Distributed in the United Kingdom by GMC Distribution Services
Castle Place, 166 High Street, Lewes, East Sussex, England BN7 1XU
Distributed in Australia by Capricorn Link (Australia) Pty. Ltd.
P.O. Box 704, Windsor, NSW 2756, Australia

Design by Andrea Miller
Art by Jen Taylor

For information about custom editions, special sales, and premium and corporate purchases,
please contact Sterling Special Sales at 800-805-5489 or specialsales@sterlingpublishing.com.

Manufactured in China
Lot #:
2 4 6 8 10 9 7 5 3 1
12/15

www.sterlingpublishing.com/kids

CONTENTS

What's that smell?

There's no getting around it—garbage stinks. Back in the olden days, before there were big garbage trucks, trash was collected in wagons pulled by horses. When you heard the call, "Here comes the garbage man!" it was time to run inside and close the windows. That wagon stank! But why? Where do those smells come from?

Garbage smells bad because of very, very tiny creatures called bacteria. Bacteria are single-celled living things, and they are all around you. Even though bacteria are too small for you to see without a microscope, they are very important. Bacteria eat and break down food. In fact, bacteria even live inside of you and help you get energy from the food you eat. You can *smell* the bacteria when they break down old food. While they eat, bacteria give off gases like methane, sulfur, and nitrogen. It takes millions of bacterial cells to eat, or decompose, food. They can make quite a stink, but without bacteria, old food and waste would just pile up and never go away.

Thanks to bacteria, a banana peel decomposes in just two to five weeks. An orange peel gets broken down in about six months. Bacteria are nature's garbage collectors. But that doesn't mean you want to smell what they're up to. So we put our garbage in cans and close the lid. We move it to the garage or the curb, so we don't have to see it or smell it.

Of course, people throw away more than just food. People throw away paper, old furniture, broken toys, and anything else they don't want anymore. In much of the world, people are hired to work in sanitation. It is the sanitation department's job to take away garbage and sort it. While it's easy to throw something away, the journey garbage takes only just begins when it's tossed into a trash bin.

Why do we throw garbage away at all?

Sanitation means keeping things clean. By taking garbage away, sanitation workers help keep cities clean. In places without sanitation, garbage piles up. Bacteria growing on garbage may make people sick, and the smell of trash attracts rats, flies, and other things that people don't want around. By putting trash in garbage cans, we "contain" it, so it doesn't make a big mess on the street. And by removing it, we keep people healthier.

Back before there were laws against it, people threw food, garbage, and fireplace ashes out into the street. This attracted rats, roaches, and even pigs. These animals made the mess even messier. Bacteria breaking down garbage could get into the water supply and make people sick. Rats carry diseases too. So collecting garbage and keeping it off the street not only makes living in the city nicer, it makes it safer too. Without a sanitation department, life in the city would be almost impossible.

But even with sanitation departments, some garbage still ends up on the streets today. We call it litter. Litter makes cities dirty and feeds those pesky rats and flies. It can also make animals sick or hurt plants. While food might attract bugs and animals, other things we throw away can be harmful. Batteries have chemicals that are dangerous to nature. Paper and plastic take a long time to break down. Sometimes animals eat plastic thinking that it is food.

We throw garbage away to keep clean. But we are making and throwing away too much. Americans throw away enough garbage every day to fill 63,000 garbage trucks. Each American throws away an average of 4.5 pounds (2 kilograms) of garbage a day, and it adds up to more than 1,640 pounds (745 kg) every year. In Europe, people seem to throw away much less. The average German person only produces an average of just below 1,000 pounds (450 kg) of garbage per year. We're throwing out more than ever! And that is not a good thing.

The same street in New York City—before and after sanitation.

How can we make less garbage?

If we don't want our planet to become a giant trash heap, we need to remember three words: *reduce, reuse,* and *recycle.*

These three *R* words are said in this order for a reason. The best thing we can do to keep our planet healthy is just make less garbage. By using fewer bags, cans, and other things that we throw away, we will make less waste. That's the "reduce" part. It takes so much energy and material to create every single plastic bag. When it gets tossed out, even more energy is used to take it away.

One easy way to reduce trash is to buy items with less packaging. You can also buy bigger portions of food at the supermarket and then store it in smaller, reusable containers. This will cut down on packaging that has to be thrown away. Buy fresh fruit and vegetables that don't come in packages at all. They're healthier too! You can save energy and stop creating so much waste just by not buying or using unnecessary things.

Another good way to make less garbage is to reuse things you already have. Reusing goes hand in hand with reducing how much you buy or use. And even if you don't need something anymore, someone else might. If you're too big for your old clothes, but they're still in good shape, give them to a friend or donate them to charity. If you get a new bike, you can give your old one to a younger brother or sister. When you don't need this book anymore, you can donate it to a library or a bookstore!

Finally, recycle. When you can't reuse something, see if you can recycle it. Recycling is the process of breaking down an old thing and using the parts to make something new. Glass, paper, and metal can all be recycled. So before you throw anything away, it's very important to find out if you can recycle it.

Where do garbage trucks go?

Not everything can be reused or recycled. So where does garbage go when it is thrown away? First, a sanitation worker collects the trash, tossing it into a garbage truck. Next, it's delivered to a sorting facility. There, any material that can be reused gets separated from what can't. Glass, metal, plastic, paper, and paper products like cardboard can all be reused. It helps to separate these recyclables from trash before you take them out for pickup. Recycling can be very complicated. Even different types of metal need to be sorted from one another before they can be recycled. This is a lot of work.

Garbage that can't be recycled is grouped together. Bacteria that break down garbage produce both gas and some liquid we call garbage water. All the liquid must be drained. People who throw away cups or bottles with liquid still in them are adding to the garbage water. It's important to empty a bottle completely before throwing it in the recycling bin.

Collecting garbage is a smelly job. Garbage trucks can carry more than eight tons of waste at once. If one trash bag smells bad, imagine how bad a whole truck full of hundreds of garbage bags must stink! That's a lot of trash. But after garbage is collected, sorted, and drained, what happens to it?

Garbage and recycling materials are separated at huge sorting facilities. If everyone separated their recycling and garbage before putting trash out to be collected, the recycling process would be much easier.

What is a landfill?

Whatever doesn't get recycled goes to a landfill. A landfill is a place where garbage gets buried. Most cities have their own landfills. Many landfills start as a big hole. The bottom and sides of the hole are covered in clay and a layer of plastic. This keeps any harmful or dangerous liquids and chemicals from leaking into the ground. Pipes and a layer of rocks are put down next, to catch any of that liquid.

Garbage is thrown into the landfill's pit and packed into place by bulldozers, so it takes up as little room as possible. Every day the garbage is covered in a layer of dirt. This is to keep the garbage from blowing away in the wind and also to keep rats and other pests from getting into it. Layer by layer, the landfill's pit is filled in, until the pit is full.

What can we do with landfill land?

Sometimes we make and fill landfills to actually build more land. It sounds crazy, but it's true. Parts of New York City were actually once a landfill. If you walk around the city, you would never know where the land stops and the landfill begins. Parts of downtown Chicago and the Marina District of San Francisco were also built on landfill. Other things are built on landfill too: golf courses, parking lots, and even stores. Chambers Gully in Adelaide, Australia, is now a beautiful park full of trees and koalas. You'd never know part of it used to be a landfill!

It takes a lot of planning before a landfill can be turned into something else. A cover needs to be put over the waste and dirt. As the bacteria break down food and other waste, they produce gases like carbon dioxide and methane. Methane is explosive and can be dangerous. To close up a landfill for good, pipes have to be put in to let the gases escape. Some of those gases can be burned to make electricity. In Mexico City, a power plant is being built on the Bordo Poniente landfill, and it will be able to power 35,000 homes with electricity.

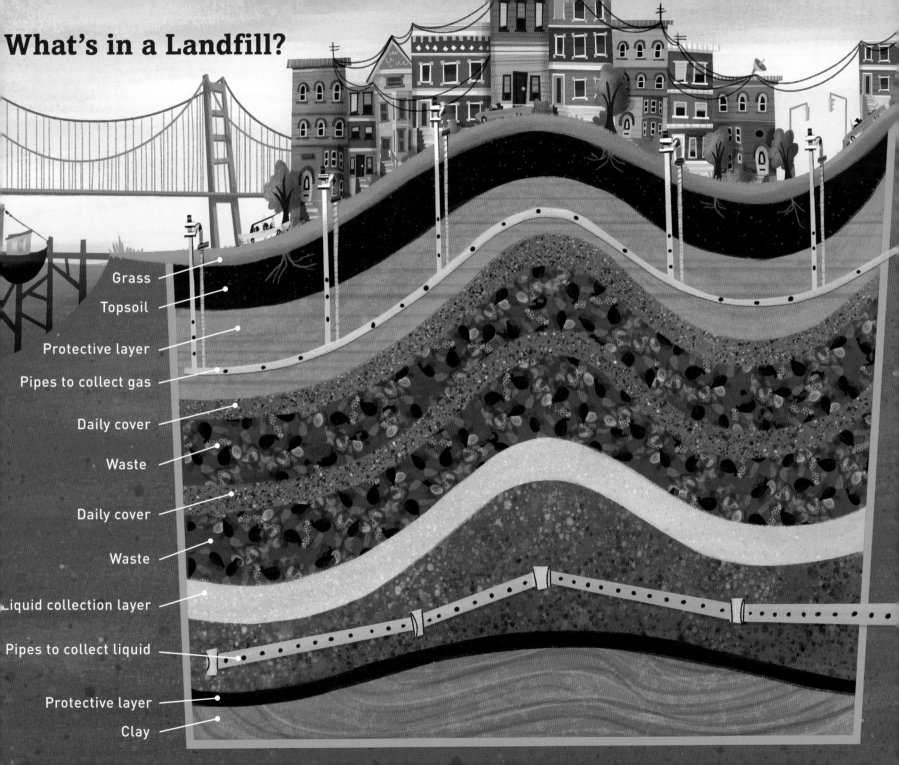

What's in a Landfill?

Grass

Topsoil

Protective layer

Pipes to collect gas

Daily cover

Waste

Daily cover

Waste

Liquid collection layer

Pipes to collect liquid

Protective layer

Clay

Why did some of New York City's garbage travel 6,000 miles?

I n 1987, New York City loaded up a big boat, called a barge, with 3,000 tons of garbage. The barge was named the *Mobro 4000*, and it was being sent down to North Carolina. New York City was running out of space in its own dumps on Staten Island. It was becoming difficult to keep garbage out of the underground water supply. If the garbage and water mixed, the city's drinking water could become polluted and make people sick. So, the city sent its garbage to other places with more room.

The state of North Carolina had accepted New York's garbage before, but this time, they didn't want the *Mobro 4000*'s trash. A picture of the load showed a bedpan, which is used in hospitals. People were scared that there might be medical waste—old needles and medicine and bandages—on the barge. They were worried that the garbage was dangerous, so they refused the *Mobro*.

Over the next two months, the barge set off on what became a 6,000-mile (over 9,600-kilometer) journey to find a place to dump its garbage. It went to Louisiana, Alabama, Mississippi, Florida, back up to New Jersey, down to the Bahamas, over to Mexico, and all the way to Belize! No one would take the *Mobro*'s garbage. The barge eventually returned to New York, where it sat for another three months. Finally, five months after it set sail, the garbage was burned in Brooklyn and the ashes were buried on Long Island, close to New York City.

The *Mobro*'s case was unusual, and it got a lot of attention. It made cities start to rethink how they were handling their garbage. People realized they needed to be more careful with garbage, and cities started encouraging their citizens to recycle more. We only have a limited amount of space on Earth. It is our responsibility to take care of the planet for all the plants and animals on it. The less garbage we make, the more space all living things have. We need to plan carefully to close up old landfills and build new ones safely.

What makes some garbage dangerous?

So many places rejected the *Mobro*'s garbage because they were afraid that there was medical waste on board. Medical waste comes from hospitals, clinics, doctors' offices, dentists' offices, blood banks, or veterinary hospitals and clinics. It can include used bandages, rubber gloves, or single-use tools used in surgeries. There can also be needles that were used to give people shots, or vials, beakers, and other pieces of glass. This waste can carry harmful germs and diseases. It is extremely dangerous to get poked by these needles or broken glass. Not only could you get cut, but you could also get very sick.

It's important that medical waste get sorted out from the rest of the garbage. That's why doctors' offices and pharmacies have special boxes to dispose of "sharps"—old needles and syringes. That way, medical waste is disposed of properly and not grouped with the rest of the garbage.

But other types of garbage can be dangerous too. Fluorescent light bulbs—the long, white lights that you might see in stores or in school—are made of glass. This makes them sharp when the light bulb breaks, and they also have a chemical called mercury in them. Mercury can poison people or animals if it gets out. So fluorescent light bulbs must be thrown away very carefully. CFL light bulbs in your house also may contain mercury. They should not be thrown away in your normal trash. It is important to look up safe places to take these light bulbs.

When electronics, like old cell phones, computers, or TVs, get thrown away, it is called e-waste. Americans throw away over 2.4 million tons of the stuff each year. The average cell phone is thrown away after only two years. E-waste can sometimes contain harmful chemicals (in batteries, for example), so if it can't be donated, it must be thrown away properly. Many old electronics have valuable metals, like gold, silver, and copper in them. If e-waste is recycled, these metals can be removed and recycled to make new electronics or other things.

Hazardous Waste

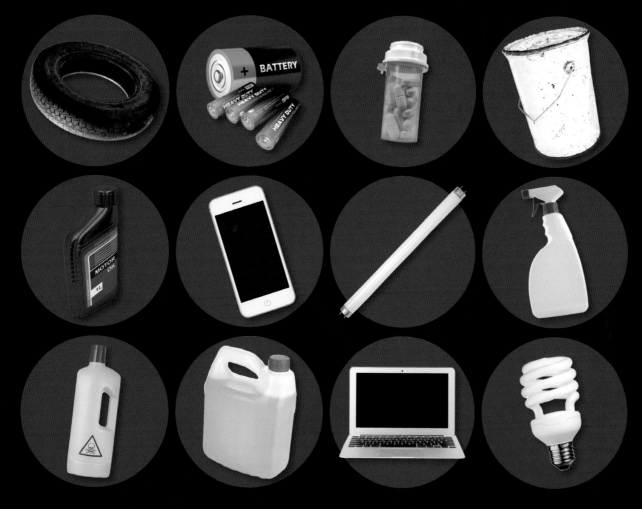

Not all garbage should be bundled together and thrown away in the same place. Medical waste, fluorescent light bulbs, CFL light bulbs, e-waste, batteries, motor oil, and cleaning products should *not* be tossed in with regular garbage.

What is the Great Pacific Garbage Patch?

Sometimes it's not just *what* the garbage is, but *where* it is that makes it dangerous. In the Pacific Ocean, 1,000 miles (1,600 km) off the coast of California, the water is very calm. There aren't many big fish or whales, but there is a huge patch of water that's cloudy and soupy because it's full of plastic. The plastic patch is twice the size of Texas! Most of the pieces of plastic are very small, the size of your thumbnail. It's the largest collection of litter in the world, and it's destroying marine life in the area.

Plastic stays in the ocean for a long time because it's waterproof and durable. Scientists think that 90 percent of the trash floating in the ocean is plastic. Researchers estimate that more than five trillion plastic particles are in the ocean. That's nearly 270,000 tons of plastic garbage! Much of it sinks all the way down and then harms life on the ocean floor.

Because the plastic breaks apart again and again, it becomes smaller and smaller. Birds and fish can mistake the tiny pieces of plastic for food. Scientists have found birds that have died with their stomachs full of plastic. If a large animal eats a smaller animal filled with plastic, that means the large animal now has that plastic in its body too. Hundreds of thousands of plants and animals die every year from garbage in the ocean. People are working hard to clean plastic out of the ocean, but more pollution is added to the ocean every day. It's important to try to use the least amount of plastic possible and to always recycle the plastic you do use. When you go to the beach, make sure to clean up after yourself. Remember to leave it better than you found it—and that means cleaner!

What are other options for getting rid of garbage?

One way we can get rid of garbage—or at least have it take up less space—is by burning it in a process called incineration.

Burning garbage produces ash that takes up 90 percent less space in the landfill. In small, crowded countries like Japan and Denmark, most of the garbage gets incinerated. It's even possible to burn garbage and use the fire to create energy: As garbage is burned, it heats water, which turns into steam. The steam turns giant turbines, making electricity. Since we use electricity for things like lights and refrigeration, this is a clever use of incineration.

Unfortunately, incineration isn't perfect. All of that burning garbage produces pollution. Incinerators pump out carbon dioxide. This gas is fine in small doses, but when we make too much, it causes global climate change. Incineration can also release dangerous chemicals like mercury into the air. The ash that is left over is much more toxic than garbage. Even if fluorescent light bulbs and other things that should not be incinerated are removed, the ash is dangerous. Building and running an incinerator can be very expensive for a city, even if it is making and selling electricity from it. The air has to be filtered to reduce pollution, and all the dangerous things that don't burn have to be sorted out.

Since garbage has to be sorted before being burned anyway, there's actually a better way to take care of garbage than incineration or landfill. It works so well companies pay for the privilege of taking a city's garbage. It's called *recycling*!

Incinerators like this one turn garbage into ash. The ash takes up less space in a landfill than the garbage would.

Why it is good to recycle?

The less garbage we make, the better. To keep the planet healthy and safe, it's important to reduce, reuse, and recycle. Recycling is better than throwing something away for many reasons. First, it keeps waste out of landfills and keeps litter off the streets. Recycling also transforms garbage into something new. This means that you don't have to cut down more trees to make more paper or mine more aluminum to make soda cans. And you can make cool new things with less trouble for the environment.

Recycling is also getting easier and cheaper. Many city sanitation departments now offer recycling—there are over 8,000 programs in the US that collect recyclables from the curb—the same way trash is collected. But instead of ending up in landfill, this trash goes to a recycling plant.

What is a recycling plant?

Most recycling plants do two major things: sort out recyclables and break them down. In order to turn something old into something new, you usually have to take it apart first. That means smashing up all the glass, melting down all the metal, and ripping up all the paper. First, the trash needs to be sorted out. There are many very clever ways of doing this. When garbage is put onto conveyor belts, magnets grab out pieces of metal, and puffs of air sort out pieces of plastic. The conveyor belt then runs at an upward angle, like going up a hill. It bounces up and down, sorting the glass and breaking it into little pieces, while also separating cardboard and paper. The broken glass falls through the conveyor belt, while the flat paper gets caught on the belt and is taken upward. Any paper or cardboard that is round, like a milk or juice carton, rolls downward and is collected.

How does an old glass bottle turn into a new one?

Paper, plastic, glass, and metal are all recycled differently. Paper and cardboard are torn into tiny pieces. Chemicals are added as cleaners, and the whole batch is turned into pulp. Pulp is used to make new paper towels, cardboard, or even books.

Glass recycles even better than paper. After being recycled a few times, paper can't be recycled again. But glass can be recycled over and over with no loss of quality. To be recycled, glass first has to be sorted by color. Then it is crushed into a fine, gritty, sand-like state called cullet. Cullet is melted back down into more glass. Recycling old glass is much better for the environment than making brand-new glass from scratch. The energy saved by recycling just one glass bottle instead of making a new one could power a light bulb for four hours.

The first step in recycling metal is to sort it by type. First, metal with iron in it, such as steel, is separated out from metal without iron. Steel doesn't wear out after being recycled many times. Cars can even be made from the recycled steel of old ovens. Once metal is sorted, it is crushed into cubes. Next, it is melted down in big furnaces. When the metal is melted into a liquid, it can be poured into new shapes. As with glass and all other recycling, making new metal out of old metal saves a lot of energy.

Plastic can be recycled into a lot of things. Polyester cloth and plastic bottles are made from the same substance, so it's possible to even make clothing or backpacks from old bottles. First the bottles are broken down into plastic pellets, or chips. Those are then spun and melted back down and drawn out in very, very small strands. Each one is five times finer than a single human hair! Then the strands are cooled and put onto giant spools that spin at 125 miles per hour (200 kilometers per hour). With a little bit more treatment to make the new yarn more pliable, the polyester fiber can be woven into fabric and become clothing.

Recycling Aluminum Cans

1

2

3

STEP ONE
Drop a used can into the recycling bin.

STEP TWO
Cans are crushed into big blocks.

STEP THREE
The blocks are melted down in a big furnace.

STEP FOUR
The melted cans are cooled and shaped into a solid block of aluminum called an ingot.

STEP FIVE
A new can is made from the recycled aluminum!

5

4

Can water be recycled?

Think of how much water you use every day: You brush your teeth with it; you take a shower or a bath in it; you drink it; you cook with it; you wash your dishes in it after eating; it's even in the toilet. The average American family uses more than 300 gallons (more than 1,000 liters) a day at home. That's a lot of water! So it should be no surprise that there is another kind of recycling: water recycling.

Earth already has a water cycle that naturally recycles water. Heat from the sun causes water to evaporate, changing it from the liquid that you can drink to a gas called water vapor. Water vapor floats up into the sky, leaving most of its impurities, like dirt or salt, behind. The now clean water vapor collects into clouds. It starts to condense, or change back into a liquid, and falls back to earth as rain or snow.

But since people can't just wait for rain to use water, scientists have learned how to recycle the water we use. It is easier and better to reuse water than to collect fresh batches from rain. Once water goes down the drain in the sink, tub, or toilet, it is treated—filtered with the help of chemicals. This process removes any solid waste, or big bad impurities, like poop! Water that has been treated even just a little bit is safe to be returned outdoors. It can also be used on crops that need water to grow. The less water we have to take from rivers, wells, and lakes, the better. Treated water can also be *added* to groundwater, where it may have been taken from in the first place!

Just as with other resources, it is better to reduce the amount of water you use than to recycle it. Remember to fix leaks and drips, turn off the faucet as you brush your teeth, and consider taking a shower instead of a bath.

Water treatment plants like this one make recycled water safe to use.

Can you recycle food?

Sort of. You obviously don't want to eat old carrots once they've gone bad, or rotten fruit or moldy bread. But you know who might want to eat that expired food? Worms! And bacteria! In fact, bacteria eating this food is what's making it go bad in the first place. It's what turns a delicious banana into something far from tasty. But it's a good thing we have worms and bacteria. We don't want the world to fill up with all those old lunches, do we? What's really cool is that once food is broken down, what's leftover is a great fertilizer. You can even put the fertilizer in your garden to help plants grow! This process is called composting.

By composting, you reduce the amount of garbage that goes to the landfill, is incinerated, or ends up becoming litter. And it's fun to do! You can make a compost bin for your family's old food or even as a class project.

To compost, all you need is a little bit of outdoor space, or room for extra garbage in your yard. You can also use a garbage can with the bottom cut off and some airholes on the side. Or you can build a compost bin out of wooden slats or chicken wire held in place with stakes in the ground if you're feeling ambitious.

Once your compost bin is built, start adding grass cuttings, leaves, flowers, vegetable scraps, fruit scraps and peels, table scraps, eggshells, coffee grounds, and stale bread to your compost pile. Paper, cardboard, sawdust, animal manure, and seaweed can also be composted. A good rule to remember is to have lots of greens and browns. You want a mix. If you want things to decompose faster, you can shred whatever you're putting into it—especially brown paper products, because otherwise they take a looooong time! Don't put in meat or dairy products, like cheese. These take a long time to break down and can smell very bad and attract rats. With care, your compost heap will decompose into nice, rich soil that can be used in the garden.

Compost Bin

Brown leaves

Kitchen scraps

Straw

Grass clippings

Brown leaves

Green leaves

Sticks

What can we do to help?

People are making too much garbage! It's bad for the environment and dangerous for the planet. But you can help! The best thing you can do is make less trash. That means buying things that will last longer. Buying used things from thrift stores or online makes a big difference too. Another way you can help is by making sure you take a reusable cloth bag with you to the supermarket or the store, so that you don't have to use a plastic or paper bag.

Another big problem is water bottles. Americans use sixty million plastic water bottles every day! It's estimated that it takes up to 700 years for plastic bottles to break down and decompose. It also takes fifteen to seventeen million barrels of oil to make, transport, and throw away all those bottles every year. Most of the time, bottled water isn't any better than water from the faucet! Instead of buying or grabbing a new bottle of water whenever you are thirsty, get a reusable one. You can buy a durable water bottle once and use it for, well, 700 years! If we all do our best to reduce garbage, the planet will be a much better place.

FIND OUT MORE

Books to read

Ganeri, Anita. *Something Old Something New. Recycling.* Chicago: Heinemann Raintree. 2005.

Hunter, Rebecca. *Waste and Recycling.* North Mankato, Minnesota: Sea to Sea Publications, 2012.

Parker, Victoria. *Helping the Environment.* Chicago: Heinemann Raintree. 2012.

Ward, D. J. *What Happens to Our Trash?* New York: HarperCollins. 2012.

Wilcox, Charlotte. *Earth-friendly Waste Management.* Minneapolis: Lerner Publishing Group. 2009.

Winter, Jonah. *Here Comes the Garbage Barge.* New York: Schwartz & Wade. 2010.

Websites to visit

Kids Be Green
http://www.kidsbegreen.org/
Facts, coloring sheets, and games

National Institute of Environmental Health Sciences—Kids' Pages
http://kids.niehs.nih.gov/explore/reduce/
Listen to songs, read tips on recycling, and more.

Meet the Greens
http://www.meetthegreens.org/
Funny videos and games about how our actions impact Earth

PBS Kids It's My Life, Green Living
http://pbskids.org/itsmylife/family/greenliving/
Tips and links to teach you how to shop better and care for the environment

Recycle City
http://www3.epa.gov/recyclecity/
Learn what recycling looks like for an entire small town

For bibliography and free activities visit: http://sterlingpublishing.com/kids/good-question

INDEX